Larry Burkett's
Consumer Books For Students

getting *your* first credit card

Larry Burkett
with **Ed Strauss**

Illustrated by **Ken Save**

MOODY PRESS
CHICAGO

Text & Illustrations © 2000 BURKETT & KIDS, LLC

Larry Burkett's Money Matters For Kids
Executive Producer: *Allen Burkett*

For Lightwave Publishing
Managing Editor: *Elaine Osborne*
Project Assistant: *Ed Strauss*
Text Director: *Christie Bowler*
Art Director: *Terry van Roon*
Desktop Publisher: *Andrew Jaster*

Special thanks to Bill Wise for producing the charts on page 35 and 36.

ISBN: 0-8024-0979-2

1 3 5 7 9 10 8 6 4 2

Printed in the United States of America

table of
contents

how to use
this book

Shortly after leaving home, many teens and young adults embark on a learning curve so drastic that it resembles a roller-coaster ride. Things they never did before—such as operating a washing machine, paying bills, shopping for groceries, renting an apartment, using a credit card—suddenly become sink-or-swim survival skills. Most teens fail to learn these basics while still at home and are woefully unprepared for life in the real world when they move out on their own.

The four books in this series—*Getting Your First Credit Card*, *Buying Your First Car*, *Renting Your First Apartment*, and *Preparing For College*—were written to fill these gaps in modern education and to teach you the basic life skills you need to survive in today's jungle. In this series we walk you step-by-step through buying a used car without being conned, using a credit card without diving into debt, going to college without mortgaging your future away, and renting an apartment without headaches.

These books contain a wealth of commonsense tips. They also give sound advice from a godly, biblical perspective. It is our prayer that reading the books in this series will save you from having to learn these things in the school of hard knocks.

To get the most out of these books, you should photo-copy and complete the checklists we've included. They're provided to help you take on these new tasks step-by-step and to make these books as practical as possible.

Each book contains a glossary to explain commonly used terms. If at any point while reading you need a clear definition of a certain word or term, you can look it up. Each book also contains a helpful index that allows you to find every page where a key word or subject is mentioned in the book.

chapter one

what is a ***credit*** card

what is a
credit card?

A credit card is a piece of plastic 2 1/8" x 3 3/8" with a magnetic strip about 6/16" wide going across the back. OK, so that's not telling you a whole lot. Actually, it is. A credit card is that particular size to make sure it fits in your wallet so that you'll carry it around with you everywhere you go and use it often. And the magnetic strip is there so that when cashiers swipe it on their machine in a department store, they can electronically connect with the company that issued the card to be sure you have sufficient credit to make your purchase.

A credit card can be a great convenience, one of the wonders of our modern age, but only as long as you faithfully pay your statements at the end of each month, in full. Let your bills get out of control, however, and a credit card becomes a monster that threatens to destroy you and all you hold dear.

debit cArd, creDit card, oR cHarge caRd?

A credit card is not the same thing as a debit card. A debit card (or bank card) allows you to make purchases by electronically withdrawing money you have deposited in a bank account. As long as there's still money in your account, your debit card works fine.

The second your money runs out or you go to make a $49.99 purchase and only have $11.32 left in checking, the bank card doesn't work. The clerk turns to you and says, "Sorry. It says *Insufficient Funds*." You try again. This time when the machine asks, "Which account?" you hit *Savings*. Bummer. *Insufficient Funds* again.

At this point, most Americans pull out their credit card. A credit card is a different animal. It allows you to spend money you don't have. Owning a credit card with a line of credit for $2,000 is like having standing permission to borrow up to $2,000 to buy whatever you want, whenever you want. Now, if you foolishly charged your credit card to the max, the clerk will inform you that *it* has not been accepted either. Your face goes red at this third public declaration of bankruptcy, and the people in line behind you are beginning to grumble.

You wisely guess that the cashier won't accept your Fill'ErUp charge card—since that only works at Fill'ErUp gas stations—so you pull out *another* credit card muttering, "This one should work." To your relief, it does. You hastily grab your $49.99 purchase and head for the door.

A charge card is similar to a credit card except you're required to pay off your total purchases in full at the end of each month. Gas station chains used to issue charge cards to regular customers, but most of them have since found it more profitable—*far* more profitable—to issue regular credit cards and charge you 24 percent interest or more.

whence tHe creDit meNtaliTy?

Credit cards have become a permanent fixture of modern society, but they have not been around since the dawn of civilization. In fact, living on credit is a rather recent concept. For centuries, American presidents understood clearly that the government treasury should not be used to supply public needs. They also understood the need for a balanced budget. In other words, the government should not spend more money than it actually had.

Franklin Roosevelt changed all that. In 1932 he campaigned under the banner of more government intervention in the economy. Nevertheless, he did promise to balance the budget. In 1938, however, he followed the advice of

John Keynes, a British economist whose basic idea was that deficits were good, that to keep people fully employed, governments *had* to run up debts and spend more money than they had.

The government began living on credit, laying the foundation for the present debt mentality. For most Americans, however, things still worked on a "cash only" basis. In the 1950s a person could not qualify for and receive a credit card unless he or she made a very healthy income. Now credit cards are given to high school students. A 1993 study reported that 32 percent of high schoolers and 82 percent of college students had at least one credit card. And over 50 percent of them have more credit card debt than they can pay off at the end of the month.

a bibLical pErspectiVe

Many of us see nothing strange about living in debt, making credit card payments to three or four different card-issuing companies each month. After all, don't we deserve to have whatever we want, even if we don't have money to buy it? Besides, everyone else is doing the same thing, so how could it be wrong?

On the other end of the spectrum, some Christians think that borrowing money for any reason (even making mortgage payments on a house) is unscriptural and that "owe no man any thing, but to love one another" (Romans 13:8 KJV) means never buying a thing on credit. They teach that credit is debt, which is a curse.

The truth is in neither of these extremes. More fully translated in the New International Version, Romans 13:8 reads, "Let no debt remain outstanding, except the continuing debt to love one another." In other words, Paul acknowledged that from time to time believers might have to borrow or buy on credit, but urged them to pay any debts faithfully and promptly.

While it certainly is better to be able to lend money than to have to borrow it, borrowing when we need to is not prohibited according to the Bible. Credit is not unscriptural and credit cards are not the mark of the Beast. It's when we go overboard and misuse credit that it becomes unscriptural and beastly.

In the Bible, borrowing and lending were commended as a way to help the poor. "Good will come to him who is generous and lends freely" (Psalm 112:5). "If there is a poor man among your brothers . . . be openhanded and freely lend him whatever he needs" (Deuteronomy 15:7–8). Borrowing is a scriptural principle. Even Nehemiah loaned money and grain to the poor during a famine, though he didn't charge interest (Nehemiah 5:1–10).

The modern concept of debt and credit, however, is the reverse of God's system. Borrowing was not used as a way to finance exorbitant lifestyles or to live on credit, which is today's main use. We want things now and give little thought to whether we'll be able to pay our credit card back or not. We want luxuries we don't need and can't afford, so we borrow the money to pay for them. This was *not* what God had in mind when He urged believers to "freely lend."

creDit wHere cRedit iS due

We're a nation that lives in debt. A recent report stated that consumer debt has reached the one trillion dollar stage, and that more than one third of that is bank credit cards, up 212 percent in the last ten years. And it's no surprise that with so much credit available, the total amount of purchases has quadrupled to almost $884 billion dollars.

There's an old joke that says, "You really have to give the American people credit. After all, if you didn't, how would they live?" We live in a credit- and debt-oriented society where having debts and paying high interest rates is the "norm," where learning how to use a credit card wisely and stay out of debt is almost a lost art. "Buy now, pay later" is a relatively new concept, but has fast become a central pillar holding up the American dream, easily replacing the old concept of saving to buy what we want.

two pOints oF vIew

The purpose of a credit card, from the point of view of many consumers, is to buy what we want now, obtain instant gratification, own the latest and the best (after all, "we deserve it"), dine out every day, and pay for it tomorrow. The mistaken thought that best describes this point of view is, "Let us eat and drink, for tomorrow we die" (1 Corinthians 15:32).

The purpose of a credit card, from the point of view of most credit card companies, is to get the consumers to borrow more than they can repay, to buy more than they need, so they end up paying exorbitant interest charges each month while slaving away to pay back the original loan. The verse that best describes this point of view is, "The borrower is servant to the lender" (Proverbs 22:7).

chapter two

curse *or* blessing?

curse or
blessing?

a tEn-ToN truCk

Since more than half of the people who own credit cards have racked up debts and are paying exorbitantly high interest rates, the question begs to be asked, "Are credit cards a blessing or a curse?" Would we all be better off if every credit card in the world was recalled and put through the shredder?

It depends on how we use them. The card itself is not bad, just as a ten-ton truck is not bad. It all depends on who's behind the wheel, whether they're cautious or reckless. Owning a credit card but having no self-restraint and no knowledge of the dangers of credit is like driving a semi with no brakes and no steering wheel. The question is not *if* it will crash, but *when.*

Many of today's twenty-somethings are carrying a huge load of debt. One of the defining characteristics of Generation Xers may be, in fact, the amount of debt they carry. Between 1990 and 1995, the *average* outstanding credit card balance of households headed by someone under twenty-five grew from about $900 to $1800. It doubled! Having access to instant credit started out as a blessing to millions of young adults, but quickly developed into a snare and a curse.

And while you may not be a Gen Xer—if you were born in 1979 or later, you're part of Generation Y—it pays huge dividends to learn the lessons of Generation X whose continuing five-year mission seems to be to explore new lines of credit and to boldly charge more on their cards than anyone has charged before.

the teMptationS

How did we get to this state? There are two trends w]
have come together to alter our behavior: the increase in
student loans and the abundance of credit cards. We have
become accustomed to easy student loans to finance our
education, and we have no problem whatsoever using credit
to pay for comfort or even our luxury items.

One of the reasons for all this borrowing and debt
may lay in our image consciousness. We want to attain
and have the lifestyles we see on television. We want the
fabulous apartments, the fashionable clothes, and the
trendy friends. But the only way we can achieve that level
of luxury is through the use of credit, since it's way
beyond our income.

payiNg wIth plAstic

The banks know this. They know that young adults, if they
get credit cards, will probably max them out, go in debt,
and end up paying off high interest charges. So what do
they do? Make it more difficult to get credit? No! They
make it easier. They hand them out like candy. When we're
eighteen and entering college, often the first thing we see as
we enter the doors are tables full of credit card applications.

The result? Eighty-two percent of all college students
now have credit cards. Is that good or bad? Well, of the
debtors seeking help with the National Consumer Credit
Counseling Service, *more* than half of them now are
between the ages of eighteen and thirty-two. And student
loans? In the '90s alone, students borrowed nearly two hundred billion dollars! A lot of them will be in their midthir-
ties before they finally pay those loans off.

It's not just teens who are recklessly playing with plastic. Adults are leading the pack. In fact, the record for racking up credit card debt was set by Elton John, who racked

up an incredible $40,000,000 on credit! That is a world record, apart from entire nations who borrow money to finance agricultural programs.

diVine inTerveNtion?

While credit may be hard for some people to obtain, for most it's as simple as going to their mailboxes. Even many Christians think that the arrival of a credit card is "divine intervention." We claim God "miraculously helped us" by sending us a credit card with a large cash advance to pay off all our other debts. *Hello?*

One Christian who was living off his credit cards praised God for providing another credit card just when the ones he had been using were becoming overdue. If that's not the height of arrogance and presumption, it comes pretty close.

beneFits anD bLessIngs

If we know how to handle a credit card wisely, there are a lot of benefits in owning one. It can be a blessing and a great convenience, and safer than carrying around huge wads of cash. (Although, having huge wads of cash is a problem most of us could learn to live with.)

But here are the ground rules: We have to (a) know how to live within a budget, (b) discipline ourselves to actually do it, (c) refuse to give in to impulse buying (a last-minute purchase that was not in our budget), and (d) never spend more money on credit than we can pay back in full, and on time, at the end of the month.

If we can do these four things, we'll have every convenience of owning a card, but never pay a dime in interest. But if we fall down in even *one* of those areas, we'll be dinged for more than dimes and dropped into debt.

the benefits of credit cards

Chapter Three

the benefits of
credit cards

a linE of cRedit

One of the biggest benefits of owning a credit card is that we can have an instant line of credit ranging from $500 to $50,000 (or more) without carrying thousands and thousands of dollars around in our pockets. If we're on a major shopping trip or on vacation or doing business abroad, that small plastic card can come in extremely handy—as long as we pay our credit card bills on time.

On the other hand, millions of us have already discovered that we have neither the knowledge nor the financial maturity to handle unlimited access to a high line of credit. If that's the case, it's better if we only carry around a debit card. It gives instant cash, but not a penny more than we have in our account.

If we can trust ourselves with a credit card, it has a lot more benefits than a bank card. If we travel a lot in our line of business, we'll find a *Visa* or *MasterCard* works just great when paying a hotel bill, but a bank card . . . *well* . . . it just doesn't quite cut it. And while a Bank of Possum Creek debit card works fine at diners in Possum Creek, try using it when on vacation in Luxembourg. Also, if we own a business and constantly order supplies and goods, one of the most convenient ways of doing that is with a credit card.

instaNt acCess

A credit card can give us not only a large line of credit, but instant access to that amount. Instead of having to carry a lot of money around—then being forced to drive home or to our bank when we run out—we can just pull out our card and "charge it."

safeR thaN caSh

A credit card is safer than cash. Let's say I lose $300 some-where downtown. Most people will claim "finders keepers." But since my name is written on my credit card, an honest person can look me up in the phone book and call me or turn it in to the bank that issued it. I can also call the card's 1-800 number to cancel it so a thief can't charge purchases on it. Even if he does use it, according to federal law the holder of a lost or stolen card need only repay the first $50 of unauthorized charges. This basically holds true around the world as well.

Debit cards are safer still, however. If I lose my debit card, it does a thief no good at *all* since he or she has no way of knowing my secret number.

insUrance aNd diSaster coveRage

A lot of credit card companies offer—even on their zero interest cards—thirty to ninety days insurance on purchases made with their credit card. If we buy a watch or a set of luggage and it's stolen, lost, or damaged within that period, we can call the company's 1-800 number to report it, and after verifying the purchase on our records, they'll reim-burse us. A lot of people have this benefit and don't even know it, so check with your company and ask them what benefits your credit card gives you.

If we're willing to pay higher annual fees—especially if we're paying $100 a year for a gold card—our card's insur-ance can reimburse the cost of some very expensive pur-chases. Plus, we'll get other benefits such as theft replace-ment, auto collision coverage, frequent flyer miles, airline disaster coverage, etc. Some reimburse what we pay for car rental insurance and give perks such as free restaurant din-ners, etc. While $100 a year in annual user's fees may seem

like a lot, it makes perfect sense for many businesspeople to
have a gold card.

pointS anD gift cErtificAtes

Most credit card companies give points when we use our
card, typically about 1 percent return on all credit card purchases. We can cash in our points and spend the gift certifi-
cates at participating stores for some goodies. The downside
is that people usually spend 20 percent more with a credit
card than they spend if they use cash, so getting 1 percent
back is really no deal. But if we use our card anyway, might
as well cash in our points!

estabLishinG a creDit ratIng

Some people use a credit card to establish a credit rating. If
it's on record that we borrowed money and faithfully paid it
back, then if we need a larger loan later on, we'll be seen as
a "good risk" and qualify for the loan.

There are other ways of establishing a credit rating,
however. For example, we have $1,000 in a savings account,
and then apply for $1,000 dollars on a low-interest loan.
Almost any bank will lend us $1,000, using the savings as
collateral. Then we can turn around and immediately pay
back the loan with our savings, Usually, the lender will
charge from 1 to 2 percent more for the loan than the pre-
vailing savings rate. So, in essence, it costs about 2 percent
interest to establish a credit history. For a one-year loan of
$1,000, the net cost of establishing a credit rating would be
about $20.

betwEen paychEcks

Most Americans live from one paycheck to another and
have little or no money in savings. Instead of a savings
account in which we actually save money, it's treated like a
backup checking account. But what happens when unex-

pected expenses hit and our savings account is empty too? If you remember the story at the beginning of this book about the $49.99 purchase, this is about the time that most of us pull out our credit cards.

When we're broke and between paychecks, we may be mighty thankful for a credit card to tide us over. But this is *no* way to live. When our finances are stretched so thin, all it takes is one more bill to overextend our credit and push us over the edge into debt. Instead of being glad for a credit card, we need to seriously consider changing our spending habits.

in conClusiOn

Credit cards, burden or blessing? It's up to us. If we can control credit, it can be a tremendous blessing and convenience, especially as we become adults and enter the world of business. If we can't control our card, it's time to get out the sheep shears. Why sheep shears? Read on.

chapter four

the dangers ***of credit*** cards

the dangers of
credit cards

the pUrsuIt of hAppineSs

A basic premise in the Constitution is that Americans have the right to "life, liberty, and the pursuit of happiness." That has changed in recent years. Now most us think it says, "life, the pursuit of happiness, and the pursuit of even more happiness." Forget liberty. We're so busy pursuing happiness and running up credit to enjoy life that we're in bondage to debt.

In themselves, credit cards are not dangerous. But because of the prevalent "I deserve it" attitude, they generally *have* been determined to be "hazardous to health." This is why debt-laden New Yorkers shove them through the shredder and strew them in the sewers. This is why cowboys in Colorado use them for rifle practice and farmers in Australia hack them up with sheep shears.

they looK gOod, bUt loOk ouT!

For every person who finally pays off their last credit card debt and vows never to live beyond their means again, ten young adults clutch their first card as they careen toward the mall. Like moths heading for a zap lamp, like lemmings hurtling headlong off the top of a fjord, they seem all but powerless to resist modern advertising.

Of course, this "gotta have it" attitude is not new. Ever since the invention of the eyeball, people have been ogling things they wanted. Three thousand years ago, King Solomon confessed, "I denied myself nothing my eyes desired" (Ecclesiastes 2:10). But you have to put that in perspective! Solomon could *afford* things. His annual income was twenty-five tons of gold (1 Kings 10:14). One gets the impression that he wasn't racking up a credit card debt.

Today, however, we still want to live like kings, or at least to have the lifestyle of the rich and famous, or—for crying out loud—we at least want to wear the latest fashions and own the new state-of-the-art gadgets. Don't have the money? No problem! Pull out the plastic.

overriDing God's wilL

One of the chief dangers of living on borrowed money is that it can allow us to override God. The Bible says, "My God will meet all your *needs*" (Philippians 4:19, italics added). In the past, when God didn't want us to have something—perhaps it wasn't good for us, or it wasn't the right timing, or maybe He planned on providing it for free—all He had to do was withhold the money. End of argument.

These days, if God doesn't provide the money for what we want to buy, all we have to do to override His veto is pull out our credit card—if we haven't already maxed it out, that is. If God had planned on providing what we needed some other way, or giving it to us as a gift, but we used credit to get it, then we missed His blessing.

spuR-of-tHe-momEnt sPendiNg

When we have no written budget to guide us, we frequently make very expensive spur-of-the-moment spending decisions. If we pass a furniture store and see a couch selling for a mere $390—but the sale only lasts two days—we buy it on the spot. A week later while resting on our new couch, we realize that we no longer have enough money to pay rent. Solution? We buy groceries and gas with our credit card and use the "real" money in the bank to pay our rent. Five months later we're still making payments with high interest charges.

patieNce, thRift, hArd woRk

Fifty years ago when people wanted to buy something, they worked hard to earn extra money and saved up a dollar at a time. Finally, the big day came when they had enough money and they went to the store, put down the cash, and bought it. Back then, the age-old virtues of patience, hard work, and thrift were deeply ingrained in American culture. Things had *value* because people didn't quickly forget how hard they had worked to earn the money and how long it took to save up enough.

These days purchases don't come with the same sense of cost. After all, what difference does it make if that item on the shopping channel costs $88 or $488 if all it costs us is $49.99 a month? When we want something, we want it now and we *get* it right now by pulling out our credit card and reading the little numbers over the phone. We do it with such a carefree attitude, with hardly a thought for cost, that one would think someone else was paying the bills. *Yeah, right.*

saviNg versUs CreDit

The great thing about saving money to buy what we want is that the whole time our money is sitting in the bank waiting to be spent, it's *earning* interest. The exact opposite happens when we buy something on credit. Not only do we miss out on the interest we could have been earning, but on top of it, we're *paying* interest for the privilege of making that purchase. So it really doesn't make a whole lot of sense or cents to buy on credit as opposed to saving and then buying.

the deBt menTalIty: "yoU desErve iT"

If the debt mentality had a spokesperson, she would stand up and tell us: "There's nothing wrong with living on borrowed cash. Racking up credit is perfectly natural. Everyone else has debts, so we might as well live that way too." This attitude is a recent one, but the scriptural principles it violates have been around for thousands of years.

An integral part of the debt mentality is the *we-deserve-it* mentality. TV commercials and magazine ads bombard our senses with a dizzying display of designer clothes, 30" TVs, stereos, sports cars, and exotic vacations, then tell us, "You *need* this! Sure, it's expensive, but get it anyway. You *deserve* it!" Hold the phone! The truth is we only really deserve what we *earn,* like respect and dollars.

Of course, the people who design those ads are aware that millions of desirous, "deserving" customers simply can't afford their product, which is why they mention that they "accept all major credit cards." What could be easier? We get instant gratification, enjoy a lifestyle wildly beyond our means, and then pay for it in installments of $98.99/month for the next four years.

payiNg inTereSt

What's wrong with living on borrowed money? The most obvious answer is if we borrow money, we have to pay interest on it. If we borrow money at an interest rate of 18 percent, for the first year and a half of a three-year loan, all we're going to be paying is the interest. We have literally paid back twice as much as we borrowed. So borrowing is expensive.

It's not just individuals who have a debt mentality. When those individuals get elected to public office, the result is a federal government that refuses to live within a budget. They overspend by borrowing money they don't have, and the national debt climbs higher and higher to where it is now: over $5 trillion ($5,610,271,697,232 and 31 cents to be exact). Since June 30, 1998, this debt increased by $171 million per day.

And interest payments? A full 23 percent of the national budget is spent on interest payments *alone*. Due to interest compounding, the total amount of the national debt interest increases by about $11,000 per second! That's $362 billion a year! The government has lost all hope of ever repaying the debt and is barely able to meet the interest payments.

addiCted tO borRowIng

For most of us, a credit card is a convenience that becomes *too* convenient and gets used far too often. We end up carrying a balance and paying larger credit card bills than we'd planned to. We may not be addicted to borrowing, but our spending is not totally under control. Then there are untold numbers of people who have *no* control over their spending at *all*. They are what we could call spendaholics, and they go shopping to relieve stress. They go to the mall and they buy something. One young woman had run up $2,000 to $3,000 worth of debt and felt so bad about it that she went to the mall to buy something.

destRuctiVe bOrroWing

If we get a loan and fail to repay it according to the terms of the agreement, the lender will pursue us until we repay the money. We'll be bombarded with phone calls and letters. The lender also will report our delinquency to credit reporting agencies, so getting another loan (or apartment or job) may become nearly impossible.

Also, to force us to repay the loan, the lender can sue us in court. The judge can make us sell things we own to repay the debt, and he or she can *garnishee* our wages, which means our employer must deduct our payments straight out of our paychecks and we only get what is left. This judgment will also show up on our credit record. If we end up in this state, we are definitely in financial bondage.

symPtomS of fInanciAl bOndage

Symptom Number 1: We can't pay our monthly bills, credit cards are maxed out, and other credit sources have been tapped out. And what's the treatment? Consolidation loans or denial. Consolidating our bills lowers the overall monthly payments and stretches the debt out for a longer time, but because we haven't dealt with the real problem, within a year or so the debts are usually back and the situation is worse than before.

Symptom Number 2: We decide more income is needed. This step seems logical because we've already tried a consolidation loan and that didn't work. So we take on a second job or start a weekend business to make more money. If we're married, the wife now goes to work. But if we haven't changed our spending habits, new income is absorbed very rapidly and the situation becomes even worse because now we're spending all the money *and* we have no time left to enjoy life *and* the wife has to work.

Symptom Number 3: "Why don't we buy something new?" Usually by this time the financial pressures are reaching a boiling point. So we buy a new car or go on a long vacation to get away from it all. But when the new bills hit we're even worse off. By this point, usually family and some well-meaning friends step in to bail us out, not realizing that they're treating the symptom, not the problem.

Symptom Number 4: Unfortunately, bankruptcy is next. Once the financial pressures build high enough, we declare bankruptcy, wipe out all these bills, and start all over again. And for young married couples, marital pressures build as well, and all too often their marriage ends in divorce. When we've worn out all our financial options—two incomes, loan consolidations, and family loans—sometimes bankruptcy or divorce, or both, seem like the only options.

Note: You may be getting married within the next few years, and if so, be advised that *the* largest cause of marriage failure today is finances. A full 80 percent of people who have divorced named this as the number one problem. We therefore strongly suggest that you and your fiancée read Larry Burkett's book, *Money Before Marriage* (available at ***www.cfcministry.org***) before you get married.

chapter five

what's in it
for the bank?

whAt? nO intErest pAymeNts?

Why would someone want to give us money? Why would a credit card company give you or me a card and say, "Here you are. Run it right up to your credit limit. And don't worry. Just pay me back at the end of the month and you won't even have to pay me a penny in interest."

Obviously, they plan to make a lot of money off us. Let's not kid ourselves: The credit card companies are in it for the money, the same as fishermen are in it for the fish. If they weren't making money off credit cards—a *lot* of money—they wouldn't be offering the service. When we borrow money, the lender expects to make a profit. It's his or her money and we're just "renting it." The way lenders "collect rent" is by charging interest. Interest is the fee for using another person's money.

When a bank gives us a simple interest loan, the procedure is very straightforward. We know ahead of time exactly how much interest we're expected to pay them. With a credit card, we start off paying *no* interest—with the idea that we will *never* pay any interest—but down the road, most of us end up paying far *more* interest than we'd ever pay on a bank loan.

an isSue oF greAt inTereSt

If we manage our financial affairs well and repay our credit card charges on time, we literally pay *no* interest. Some people go for years or even their entire life without paying a penny in interest penalties because they never run up a bill larger than they can pay at month's end, and they always pay on time.

But the issuing companies are banking on the fact that *most* of us do *not* manage our financial affairs well, and that at some point we'll charge more on our card than we can repay come month's end. Statistics show that *over half* of Americans who own credit cards end up paying a credit card debt month after month—and sometimes year after year. Paying interest penalties for that long pours huge profits into the companies' coffers.

Sorry for the disillusionment, but the banks literally *expect* us to overspend. They *know* that more than 50 percent of Americans will end up paying them interest. If they weren't earning these profits, they'd have a lot less motivation to give you and me a credit card. Their interest is in the interest, not our well-being.

calcUlatinG intErest rAtes

One of the most important questions when deciding on a credit card should be: "What is the interest rate if I carry a balance?" In other words, "What percentage will I pay in penalties if I can't pay everything off in time?" Several years ago a law was passed by the United States Congress called the *Truth in Lending Act*. It required that all interest be stated by its APR (Annualized Percentage Rate).

A lot of credit cards charge interest rates as high as 18 to 22 percent. This is fairly common. Some, however, have interest rates as low as 10 to 12 percent. Let's say we get a card where we only pay 12 percent on overdue charges. This 12 percent is called our annual percentage rate, the percentage cost of credit on a yearly basis.

add-oN inTereSt

This yearly sum is broken down to a daily sum, which in this case works out to about .0329 percent per day, or about a third of a cent on every dollar per day. That may not sound like much, but it adds up! Watch out when the fine print states "interest calculated daily." With this, we not only pay interest on the amount we owe (simple interest), but interest on the interest itself—compound interest, also called add-on interest.

Compound interest adds up slowly at first, but like a snowball rolling downhill, it steadily gains momentum and speed until it can bowl us right over. Credit card companies don't sit there figuring out our interest owed every day because they have nothing better to do! The figures they come up with are figures we will have to *pay!*

miniMum pAymeNts

Credit card companies make a great deal of money on interest payments, and the more money we owe them and the *longer* it takes us to repay them, the higher the add-on interest builds and the more we end up handing over in the long run. They're in no hurry for us to pay back our loan, and there's no ten-month repayment schedule like there is for a standard loan. The *slower* we repay, the *longer* we pay, the *more* we pay.

This is why credit card companies often have such a low repayment rate. They don't set such low minimum payments because they're trying to make life easy for cash-strapped Americans. They're trying to keep our payments low so that we pay them more over a longer period. In case you ever wondered, this is why adults often advise, "Pay *more* than the minimum payments."

how mUch mOney aRe wE talkiNg aBout?

As the following chart shows, Suzy had a $2,000 limit on her credit card and she unwisely charged it to the max. Suzy's card required her to pay 12 percent interest and her minimum monthly payment is 5 percent of her total unpaid bill. (At 5 percent, Suzy's first minimum monthly payment on $2,000 was $100. By the time she paid her debt down to $500, she was only paying $25 a month.) Since Suzy wanted to spend her money on a lot of other things besides bills, the minimum payment was all she ever paid. What Suzy didn't know was that by taking the easy way out, it would end up taking her six years and seven months to pay off her debt. By the time she finished paying, she had forked over $474.17 in interest charges—and that's assuming she never bought anything else with her credit card during that time!

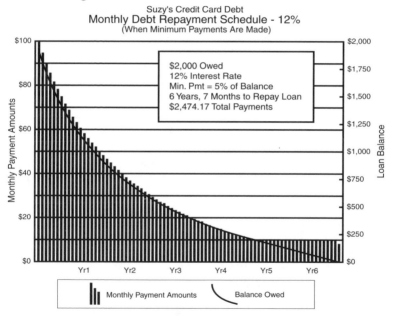

Suzy's Credit Card Debt
Monthly Debt Repayment Schedule - 12%
(When Minimum Payments Are Made)

$2,000 Owed
12% Interest Rate
Min. Pmt = 5% of Balance
6 Years, 7 Months to Repay Loan
$2,474.17 Total Payments

Monthly Payment Amounts   Balance Owed

Suzy's friend, Nadia Klug, had the exact same kind of credit card—12 percent interest with a $2,000 credit limit and a minimum monthly payment of 5 percent of her total unpaid bill. Nadia went on the same shopping binge as Suzy and maxed out her card as well. Nadia, however, decided to pay a steady $150 a month no matter what her minimum payment was. Guess what? It took Nadia only one year and three months to pay off the exact same debt, and her quick payoff cost her only $157.40 in interest, exactly $316.77 less than Suzy paid.

Joey is another matter. As you can see from the chart, his credit card charges 18 percent interest. He too racked up a $2,000 debt. Joey's minimum payment was also 5 percent of his total unpaid bill. Like Suzy, Joey decided that the minimum payment was all he would ever pay. By the time Joey finished paying his entire debt—some seven years and

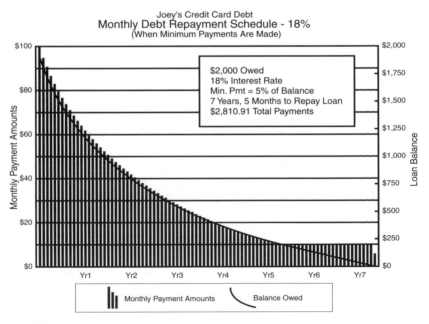

Joey's Credit Card Debt
Monthly Debt Repayment Schedule - 18%
(When Minimum Payments Are Made)

$2,000 Owed
18% Interest Rate
Min. Pmt = 5% of Balance
7 Years, 5 Months to Repay Loan
$2,810.91 Total Payments

Monthly Payment Amounts

Loan Balance

Monthly Payment Amounts   Balance Owed

five months later!—he had paid the credit card company a whopping $810.91 in interest. Now that is a *lot!*

Then there's Enrico. Like Joey, he had a credit card that charged 18 percent interest, and Enrico too ran up $2,000 in charges. Rather than making only the minimum required payments, however, he paid $150 a month. It took him one year and three months to pay off his debt, and though he paid $248.14 in interest payments (ouch!), that's still $562.77 less than Joey ended up shelling out. And Enrico only had to remember to make his payments for one year and three months, *not* seven years and five months.

Finally we come to Rob Meblind. Rob had the exact same debt—$2,000 on a credit card that charged 18 percent interest—but with a difference. Rob had a great card that only required him to pay 2.5 percent of his total unpaid debt, so Rob's required minimum payments were *much* lower than anyone else's. Rob decided to take advantage of this great deal and paid only the very low minimum payment. What someone should have explained to Rob was that this "great deal" would mean he'd take eighteen years and six months to repay $2,000, and in the end he'd have paid the credit card company $4,615.34!—an incredible $2,615.34 in interest penalties!

inteRest frOm daY oNe

OK, so we promise ourselves we'll never run up such a huge debt that it takes us months or years to repay. But here's something worth knowing if we ever fail to pay *one* month's charges in full and have to carry them over to the next month: Some people mistakenly believe that the "interest clock" only starts to tick once they receive their statement of charges and the due date passes. Wrong. The clock started to tick the moment we made those purchases, including the purchases back on the first day of the month. All that month, however, was a "grace period," and as long as we paid our account in full, on time, the interest charges didn't kick in. But miss them by one day, and suddenly all that interest hits.

Let's say one month we ran up a Visa bill of $767. If we don't pay it at the end of the month, we'll be slapped with $85 in interest penalties. Try as we might, however, the absolute most we can scrape together to pay that bill is $750. "No problem," we think, "I've paid most of it. Only $17 is carrying over into the next month. I'll probably only pay a couple dollars interest on *that*."

Surprise, surprise! If we didn't pay the *total* amount written on our bill, we are considered to have defaulted and will have to pay the *full* interest penalty of $85! Sure, it's unfair. But since most card holders don't read the fine print in their contract, they're generally not aware of this rule.

Here are a couple more areas where the companies make money on credit cards.

annuAl usEr's feE

An annual user's fee is the amount we pay the issuing bank or company each year for the privilege of having one of their cards. Depending on the kind of card we want, we could pay from $10 to $100 a year or more. If we want a basic card with no frills or benefits, we can even get cards where we pay *nothing* in annual fees. More about this later. But annual user's fees are *not* where the real money is at. It's a mere pittance compared to other ways credit card companies earn money.

profiT oN puRchaSe

One of the biggest ways credit card companies earn money is through profit on purchase. Every time we buy something with our card, the store that accepted our payment must pay the card issuer from 1.5 percent to 5 percent of our purchase price. (Huge supermarkets with high volumes of sales pay less. Small stores with low sales volume pay more.)

Let's say a small store named Frying Plans has a sale and offers Sizzle Griddles for $100 each. This is such a great price for a Sizzle Griddle that 273 people buy one. Now, if 186 of them pay with credit cards and out of that, 50 pay with an Anaconda card, how much does Frying Plans owe Anaconda Credit in one day? At 5 percent, that would be $250.

Multiply Frying Plans' sales by every other purchase made in North America that day by people using Anaconda credit cards, and every single merchant paying from 1.5 percent to 5 percent on every purchase, and you get the idea that Anaconda Credit is earning a *lot* of money without so much as raising a pinkie.

No wonder credit card companies push so hard for us to use *their* card. No wonder, even if we already have a credit card, thick application letters from credit card companies offering "special introductory rates" keep turning up in our junk mail. They can well afford to send out all that junk mail! In fact, considering the profits to be made, they can hardly afford *not* to!

Why would stores—including Frying Plans—be so willing to accept payment by credit card when they then have to pay the credit card company 5 percent on every sale? Simple! They already padded that extra 5 percent into the price they charged us. So who is ultimately paying that 5 percent to the credit card company? *We* are, every time we use our card.

Still, why would a store go through all the after-hours paperwork of credit card sales if the extra 5 percent goes to a credit card company, but *they* don't earn a penny extra? Again, it's simple. Research has shown that the same shopper will spend as high as *20 percent more* when shopping on credit than they will when shopping with cash. When the average person has to put down cold, hard cash to make a purchase, they don't spend as much.

chapter six

how to use a **_credit card_** WISELY

how to use a credit
card wisely

neeD for fInanCial eDucatIon

Most teens have a woeful lack of knowledge about credit
cards. In a high school competency test sponsored by the
Consumer Federation of America, most teens didn't know
the difference between credit, cash, charge, and debit cards.
Only 14 percent correctly identified that it was a debit card
where, upon use, funds were automatically withdrawn from
one's account. Now, 14 percent is not exactly a high score.
(Get that on your final biology exam and you'll know what
I mean.)

Furthermore, only 29 percent understood that a card
where full payment must be paid upon receipt of a monthly
statement is a charge card. A full 45 percent mistakenly
thought this was talking about a credit card. (We *should*
make a full payment upon receipt of a credit card's monthly
statement, but it is not mandatory; we are allowed to make
only a minimum payment.)

practiCing wiTh deBit cArds

Most people in America today spend more than they make,
and the only way to humanly perform such a feat is to
charge things on credit. It is therefore wise, *before* we get a
credit card, to learn not to spend one penny more than we
earn. We can do this by practicing with a debit card, also
known as a bank card.

Most Americans go through twelve years of school,
turn eighteen, graduate, and are sent out into the workplace—but unless their parents filled them in or they some-
how managed to figure it out on their own—they don't

have the first clue about living within a budget or how to safely use credit. Result? Millions of young adults end up in debt a few years after leaving high school.

Ideally, we should have opened a checking account by the time we were thirteen or fourteen, and by sixteen we should have owned a debit card and learned how to use it. Then when we were eighteen, ready to leave home and eligible for credit, we would have been prepared. One of the biggest temptations in today's society is the temptation to misuse credit, but if we learn not to spend a penny more than we have in the bank, we'll be ready.

credIt carD ruLes

Rule 1: Treat a credit card like a debit card. A debit card works only as long as we have money in our bank account. Likewise, we shouldn't charge a penny more on credit than we know we can pay in full the day our monthly statement comes in.

Rule 2: Have a budget and stick to it. Know ahead of time what we can and can't afford and never use a credit card for unbudgeted expenses. This means no "impulse buying." If we have trouble controlling our spending, we must leave our credit card at home when we head to the mall.

Rule 3: Pay credit card bills promptly. We'll pay full interest rates for any unpaid credit card debt, even if our final payment is only $2. To do this, we have to know our payment due dates. Miss by one day and we'll pay the penalty.

Rule 4: Stop using our credit card the moment we go over our limit. Admit that we can't trust ourselves with a credit card at this point in our lives. We must get out a pair of scissors, cut our card into little pieces, and then notify the credit card company. Tough advice? Sure, but it works.

Rule 5: We should pay more than the minimum payments, especially if we've racked up a debt that will take months to pay off. The longer we take to pay it off, the more hundreds of dollars we pay in interest. So we must reconfigure our budget, cut back where we can, and pay off our debt as quickly as we can.

If we abide by these five rules, we'll be spared major money trouble and credit nightmares.

chapter seven

should *you* get a *credit* card ?

should you get
a credit card?

are yoU reaDy?

If you can keep the first three credit card rules in chapter 6, you're probably ready to own a credit card. So they bear re-reading. In particular, rule number 2. It reads, "Have a budget and stick to it. . . . never use a credit card for unbudgeted expenses." If you don't have a clear idea of what a budget is or why it's important, you could end up spending all your food allowance on new scuba diving gear.

liviNg wIthin A budGet

When you're eighteen or older or have a full-time job, you should already be living within an adult budget. The form on page 52 spells out some tried-and-proven budget percentages. Photocopy it and fill it in with your actual earnings. (For more on budgeting, see the books, *Money Matters for Teens* and *Money Management for College Students*.)

You don't have a full-time job yet? Chances are good, however, that you *will* have a job sometime after graduation. What kind of job are you qualified for? What kind of wages will you earn? Even if you start at a job that pays minimum wage, you can live on that *if* you have a budget.

In the meantime, you probably do have a part-time job or receive an allowance. Even if you're operating on a simple budget (10 percent to God, 60 percent for spending, and 40 percent to savings), that's a start.

when sHoulD yoU gEt onE?

Do without credit as long as possible. The less credit you have, the less credit you are tempted to use. Many young

adults get into trouble with credit because it is easy for t..
to qualify for *more* credit than they can manage. So practice
with a debit card for now and learn to handle the responsi-
bilities. Only get a credit card when you really need one.

students aS tarGets

College-bound high school seniors are attractive targets for
credit card companies. Even if you have no established credit, lenders are eager to capture your loyalty—*and* your wallet. In fact, banks spend millions of dollars each year luring
unwary students with special promotions: no-annual-fee
cards, gold cards, frequent flyer miles, special discounts on
new cars, and other incentives. We know of a college student who obtained twenty-eight credit cards which he frequently and proudly displayed to his female friends.
Although he was only eighteen when he started his collec-
tion, by the time he had reached his twentieth birthday, he
had accumulated nearly $10,000 in debt!

A good resource for college students is Larry Burkett's
Money Management for College Students.

creDit liMits

Your initial credit ceiling will probably be $500. If you use
your card wisely, starting off with a low credit limit can be a
safeguard, allowing you to catch bad spending and bill-
paying habits and correct them early. Better to learn and
take control now before your credit limit is higher and the
consequences more serious.

A tricky thing about credit limits is that some companies automatically raise a $500 credit ceiling to $1,000 after
six months. They notify you of this at the time and suggest
you call them if you don't want a higher limit, but if you
don't read your monthly statements, you won't make the call
and the new limit kicks in. Meanwhile, you think your limit
is still $500 and accidentally charge $900 on your card. After

e companies automatically increase your limit
l there it stays unless you request a higher limit.

rAtinGs

e paying a large credit card debt month after
ing as you meet the required monthly payments,
your good credit rating is not adversely affected. But you
must make those payments. Default a few times and your
credit rating will suffer, impairing your future ability to
secure a loan, get a mortgage, etc. And it's hard to regain a
good credit standing once you've lost it. It takes a long track
record of faithful payments to finally get back in the bank's
good graces. So if you're about to default, seek help.

Where your credit rating really suffers is if you've
built up so many different debts that you can't meet the
payments and the credit card company forces you to take a
consolidation loan. The fact that they had to force you to
consolidate will appear on your record.

After this they won't trust you a whole lot with a
credit card. They may not surround your house and shout
over a bullhorn, "Miss Jones! We urge you to surrender! Lay
down your credit card . . . slowly! Come out with your
hands raised!" But they most certainly will penalize you by
giving you a restricted spending limit.

cheCking yoUr cRedit rEporT

It's wise to periodically obtain a copy of your credit report
to check it for accuracy since mistakes could cause you to
be denied a loan or mortgage. You can make a request in
writing to:

Equifax Credit Information
Service Center, PO Box 740241
Atlanta, GA 30374
1-800-685-1111
Fee: $8 for each report; less in
certain states.

TransUnionCorporation
PO Box 390
Springfield, PA 19064-0390
1-800-916-8800
Fee: $8 for an individual report;
$16 for a husband/wife report.

Experian (formerly TRW)
PO Box 2104
Allen, TX 75013-2104
1-800-422-4879 or 1-888-397-3742
Fee: $8 for each credit report
(8–10 days).

Chapter Eight

finding the *right* card

finding the
right card

chooSing a cArd

Okay, you're responsible and ready and really do need a credit card. But how do you find the right one? There are a number of different cards available. Two of the largest and better-known ones are *Visa* and *MasterCard*, and the benefit of owning one of them is that they are more widely accepted—all over the world, in fact—than cards from smaller companies.

You do want to get a credit card that is widely accepted, but you need to check out the competition, such as *American Express* and others. Your research should consist of more than just watching TV ads filled with promotions and endorsements by celebrities. You need to do some real research, check out *U.S. News & World Report*, *Money Magazine*, or *Consumer Reports*. Check your local library for copies of these magazines.

So shop around and compare the interest rates, annual fees, and services of different credit card companies, and check to be sure there will be no hidden charges applied to your monthly statements. Let's look at two of the hidden charges.

inteRest raTes

It's better to pick a card that has a 12 percent interest rate than one with a 22 or 28 percent interest rate. Clearly, this is a no-brainer. In chapter 5, beginning in the section, "Calculating Interest Rates," we explained how to choose a card with a good Annual Percentage Rate (APR). But you can choose credit cards with widely different rates from the *same* company! Rates vary not just between different companies, but according to the type of card you're getting.

anNual uSers' feEs

You can get cards where you pay $100 (or more) in annual user's fees down to $10 a year, and you can get many cards for no annual fee. If this is the case, you ask, why choose a card where you have to pay any fee? Well, cost is related to benefits. You get different cards for different needs. As explained in chapter 3, the more expensive cards carry substantial benefits, and if you're operating in a high-income bracket, those benefits can far outweigh the $100 fee.

Let's say you pay $20 in annual user's fees, but this gives you a significantly lower interest rate. Not that you're *planning* on having unpaid bills, but in case it ever happens, you'd only pay 12 percent interest instead of 22 percent interest. Later, if you rack up $4,000 in credit bills and it takes you a couple years to pay them, the decision to get the $20/year card would now save you hundreds of dollars a year. Again, when choosing a card, it's very unwise to *plan* on going into debt, but you get the picture.

anybOdy wAnt mY buSinesS?

Getting a credit card is usually not difficult. The banks *want* customers who will use the card to rack up debts and end up paying lots of interest. You may be denied by a few companies, but if you try enough places, somebody will issue you a card. Even though you have no previous credit record, some companies only require you to be eighteen, earn $100 a week, and have held your present job for the last six months.

A word of caution: If you've been turned down by a couple of companies, don't get so desperate to get a credit card that you grab the first one you're offered, even if it does have high interest rates and other bad terms. Shop until you find the kind of card you want.

Monthly Income & Expenses

Annual Income
Monthly Income   _____

LESS
1. Charitable Giving   _____
2. Tax   _____

NET SPENDABLE INCOME   _____

3. Housing (30%)   _____
   Mortgage (Rent)   _____
   Insurance   _____
   Taxes   _____
   Electricity   _____
   Gas   _____
   Water   _____
   Sanitation   _____
   Telephone   _____
   Maintenance   _____
   Other   _____

4. Food (17%)   _____

5. Auto(s) (15%)   _____
   Payments   _____
   Gas & Oil   _____
   Insurance   _____
   License   _____
   Taxes   _____
   Maint/Repair/
     Replacement   _____

6. Insurance (5%)   _____
   Life   _____
   Medical   _____
   Other   _____

7. Debts (5%)   _____
   Credit Cards   _____
   Loans & Notes   _____
   Other   _____

8. Enter. / Recreation (7%) _____
   Eating Out   _____
   Trips   _____
   Baby-sitters   _____
   Activities   _____
   Vacation   _____
   Other   _____

9. Clothing (5%)   _____

10. Savings (5%)   _____

11. Medical Expenses (5%)   _____
   Doctor   _____
   Dental   _____
   Drugs   _____
   Other   _____

12. Miscellaneous (6%)   _____
   Toiletry, Cosmetics   _____
   Beauty, Barber   _____
   Laundry, Cleaning   _____
   Allowances, Lunches   _____
   Subscriptions, Gifts   _____
     (Incl. Christmas)
   Special Education   _____
   Cash   _____
   Other   _____

TOTAL EXPENSES   _____

Net Spendable Income   _____

Difference   _____

chapter nine

credit you ***don't*** want

credit you
don't want

chucKing oFferS

Most of our problems will come from not using a credit card wisely. But sometimes using a credit card wisely can bring on problems. Like *more* credit cards! Once we have a good credit rating, word gets around and suddenly, for no apparent reason, the other companies start to follow suit and we're swamped with credit card offers. Cards with *big* credit limits!

Recently there was a man who had received no less than thirteen hundred credit cards, giving him an available credit line of more than $1,000,000. He was wise enough to use only one card and pay it off faithfully, but most of us would not be so wise and would end up with colossal debts.

If you have *one* credit card and it meets your needs, throw away the other offers. You don't need them. Or if you have one credit card (Anaconda Credit, let's say), and you're already involved in a life-and-death struggle with it and it's squeezing high interest payments out of you, *definitely* chuck any other offers. If one credit card is doing you in, why would you want more?

payiNg olD crEdit wiTh neW creDit

Some of us, however, figure that the way out of a hole is to dig ourselves in deeper. We start using a new credit card to pay off our old credit card bills. What does this accomplish? We pay off the old one, but now the new one is ticking away as the debt—plus the new interest— begins to accumulate.

If we're ever in the unenviable position where we need to consolidate our debts into one big debt so we can pay them off more easily, the thing for us to do is *not* to get a gold card with a whopping $20,000 credit limit and 18 percent interest, and use that to pay off all our debts. That would be like jumping from the frying pan into the fire. The best thing for us to do in that situation is to get a consolidation loan from a *bank,* where the interest rate is much lower.

stoRe carDs

Let's stay away from store credit cards! They have nearly as much destructive power as stepping on a land mine. Let's say that Schmop, the department store chain, offers "credit cards." They offer incentives such as points on purchases. The points are not worth a whole lot. They also give discounts on products we'd never think of buying, occasional member discounts, etc.

Hmmm. With *so* many wonderful benefits, there just *has* to be a catch. There *is*. The interest charges are outrageously high, often 24 to 28 percent! Plus, because we have a Schmop card, whenever we make a major purchase, if Schmop carries that item, we tend to shop at Schmop, hoping to get a deal. We'll get a deal, all right. If we charge a purchase on our Schmop card and don't pay it off right away, we'll have the wonderful privilege of paying 28 percent interest.

gas cArds

On our way home from Schmop with our new whatever, we stop to fill up our gas tank. There are ten gas stations along the highway, but we drive out of our way to shop at Guzzle's Gas because we have a Guzzle Gas card. "Charge it," we say as we slide our Guzzle credit card across the counter. We grin, thinking how great it is to be able to get gas all month without having to pay for it. "True," we muse, "we don't actually get any discount on the gas itself, but think of all the fun contests, lucky draws, and promos we get in on, not to mention getting candy bars at a discount. And even at 4:00 A.M. when everything's closed, some stations have pumps where we can swipe our card and still get gas."

Yes . . . there is a downside: If we fail to pay off our Guzzle card in full at the end of the month, we pay very high interest.

The only people who actually benefit from gas cards are trucking or transport companies who have several vehicles on the road. They give each of their drivers a gas card, which is fairly safe to trust someone with since they can only use it at a gas station. Then, as long as the company pays their balance each month, they're never dinged with interest. And with the high volume of gas they buy, they actually *do* get discounts on the price of gas.

chapter ten

summing *it* up

summing
it up

reaDing thE fiNe pRint

The big day has come! You've got the right card; you've
compared it to other cards and feel it's giving you the best
benefits and rates. Now what? Well, if you haven't done so
already, read the fine print. Sure, it will take time. You may
even have to phone the card-issuing company and have
them walk you through it. If it takes you two hours but
helps you avoid paying hundreds of dollars in unexpected
interest charges, it's a good investment of your time.

Once you're sure you know what you're getting into,
fill out the application form. Before a company gives you a
credit card, they're going to require some information from
you. Most of all, they're interested in knowing if you have a
steady job or not and what your income is. So when they
give you the form, you'll have to fill in the name of your
workplace, phone number, etc.

a creDit chEck

In filling out the form, you need to be aware that that little
box you just checked authorized them to do a credit check
on you. And that is exactly what they'll do next. That's why
they don't give you the credit card then and there after you
sign. They need time to check you out. If you're approved,
the rest is easy: When the card comes, sign it and put it in
your wallet or purse.

safegUarDing yOur caRd

You need to make sure you also write out the number of
your card, as well as the 1-800 number of the company that

issued it, and put that paper in a secure place with your other important papers. (Or just keep the piece of cardboard your card was attached to. All the information is there.) You should also keep the card number and 1-800 number in your wallet, separate from your credit card. Should you ever lose your card, you'll be mighty thankful you did this.

Then read this book through again and give yourself a refresher course on how to best use your new card and avoid the pitfalls.

what iF yOu loSe iT?

People sometimes misplace or lose credit cards. If you notice your card missing and a frantic search of your clothes, wallet, or purse doesn't turn it up, try to remember where you last used it. If you're not used to using it, you may have forgotten to take it back after a transaction.

Check your receipts for the phone number of the last place you were at and call them. If you also forgot to claim your receipt (what a day!) look up their number in the phone book. If the store says they have it, tell them you'll be there right away. If they don't have it, consider your card lost or stolen.

At this point, dig out your card number, phone the company, tell them your card is missing, and ask them to put a "hold" on it. This will immediately make your card useless. When a thief tries to use it, he won't be able to. Don't worry—if you find your card in your pocket five minutes later, you can always call the company back, tell them it's been a crazy day, and ask them to activate it again. They won't mind. Or if they do, they won't say so.

when sOmeonE uSes yoUr numBer

Your card may be safely in your purse or wallet and someone may still be using it to rack up bills for hundreds of dollars. After all, when ordering merchandise over the phone, you have to give your name and card number. That's all a thief has to overhear. Or perhaps an unscrupulous salesclerk or cashier copied your name and number off a receipt. Recent documentaries have exposed how expert thieves gather hundreds of names and credit card numbers by listening in on analog cell phone calls.

This is why it's important to check the itemized list of purchases on the statement of charges that the credit card company mails you. If you see a purchase—or several purchases—that you know you didn't make, something is amiss. And be warned: Thieves who use others' credit card numbers often don't make several huge purchases at once. That would immediately get your attention. Instead, they make smaller purchases from time to time in the hopes you don't bother to check and won't notice.

Be aware of identity scams as well. Don't ever give out your Social Security number, or someone can assume your identity, rack up bills in your name, and ruin your credit history.

finAnces aNd thE calL of God

Finally, let's put it all in perspective. God has great plans for each of our lives, and though He has endowed each one of us with a goodly portion of human wisdom, only He is way out there ahead of us all and can see the whole game plan. Only of God can it be said, "his understanding has no limit" (Psalm 147:5). This is why we are instructed in Psalm 37:5, "Commit your way to the Lord." God knows best, and if we yield our hearts and plans to Him, obey His Word, and let Him lead us, life can be very fulfilling and full of joy.

An integral part of obeying God and seeking His highest will for our life is to "put [our] house in order" (Isaiah 38:1), and this includes not only spiritual matters, but financial. One of the greatest heartbreaks for young men or women sincerely desiring to serve God is to realize that because they didn't manage their finances properly and they're now in debt, they're not able to respond to God's call in their life.

If God calls them to go to Bible school but they just took out a loan on a shiny new car, they can't go till the loan is repaid years later. If God calls them to teach in a Christian school (a low-paying job, by the way), they have to take a higher-paying job instead in order to pay off their debts. If God calls them to the mission field, they can't go until they're debt free.

Jesus said, "If you hold to my teaching, you are really my disciples. Then you will know the truth, and the truth will set you free" (John 8:31–32). Jesus wants us to be free spiritually *and* free from debt, free to follow Him wherever He leads. Handling credit wisely is therefore not a mundane, unspiritual matter. It is an integral part of living for Jesus.

Glossary

Annual Percentage Rate (APR): The amount of interest you pay each year on all unpaid credit card bills—e.g., 12 percent interest.

Annual user's fees: Money paid each year for the privilege of owning a credit card.

Bank card: A card issued by banks which allows you to withdraw money from your bank accounts and make purchases at stores with Interact machines.

Budget: A specific, written plan where you allot a percentage of your income to each category of bills and expenses.

Charge card: Like a credit card, but only valid in certain stores; must be paid in full every month.

Compound interest: Interest which is calculated daily (based upon the APR). It is interest upon the interest.

Credit card: A plastic card issued by a bank or credit card company, which gives you instant access to a set amount of money.

Credit limit: The total amount of money you're allowed to charge on your card.

Debit card: (See Bank card)

Interest: Money you pay for the privilege of borrowing money.

Line of credit: (See Credit limit)

Minimum monthly payment: The least amount you can pay on a credit card bill without becoming delinquent.

Statement of charges: The papers your credit card issuing company sends you every month, telling the total amount you owe them, the due date, etc.

Index

Larry Burkett's Money Matters for Kids™ is providing practical tips and tools children need to understand the biblical principles of stewardship. **Money Matters for Kids™** is committed to the next generation and is grounded in God's Word and living His principles. Its goal is *"Teaching Kids to Manage God's Gifts."*

Money Matters for Kids™ and **Money Matters for Teens™** materials are adapted by **Lightwave Publishing™** from the works of best-selling author on business and personal finances, **Larry Burkett.** Larry is the founder and president of **Christian Financial Concepts™**, author of more than 50 books and hosts a radio program "Money Matters" aired on more than 1,100 outlets worldwide. **Money Matters for Kids™** has an entertaining and educational website for children, teens, and college students, along with a special **Financial Parenting™** resource section for adults.

Visit **Money Matters for Kids** website at: **www.mmforkids.org**

building Christian faith in families

Lightwave Publishing is a recognized leader in developing quality resources that encourage, assist, and equip parents to build Christian faith in their families.

Lightwave Publishing also has a fun kids' website and an internet-based newsletter called *Tips & Tools for Spiritual Parenting.* This newsletter helps parents with issues such as answering their children's questions, helping make church more exciting, teaching children how to pray, and much more.

For more information, visit Lightwave's website: **www.lightwavepublishing.com**

The Name You Can Trust®
A MINISTRY OF MOODY BIBLE INSTITUTE

Moody Press, a ministry of Moody Bible Institute, is designed for education, evangelization, and edification.

If we may assist you in knowing more about Christ and the Christian life, please write us without obligation:

Moody Press, c/o MLM Chicago, Illinois 60610
Or visit us at Moody's website:
www.moodypress.org